The Ultimate Guide To Party Shot Recipes

Roberta .E Craft

Introduction

This book offers a delightful journey into the world of creative and engaging shots, perfect for those venturing into mixology or looking to spice up their gatherings. Starting with Jell-O shots like the Apple Cinnamon Party Shots and moving into gourmet delights such as the Buttery Nipple Gourmet Pudding Shots, the cookbook presents an array of options that blend the joy of desserts with the excitement of spirited drinks. These recipes cleverly mimic favorite treats, such as the Black Forest Cake and Key Lime Pie, in a sippable form, adding a touch of novelty to familiar flavors.

Beyond the realm of gelatin and pudding, the collection expands into a more traditional but equally inventive array of shots. Classics like the B-52 Bomber find their place alongside playful concoctions such as the Brain Hemorrhage, showcasing the versatility and creative potential of shot making. The cookbook doesn't shy away from the bold and adventurous, with recipes for the Jager Bomb and Kamikaze Shots encouraging a lively atmosphere at any party.

For those with a sweet tooth, the transition from liquid desserts to spirited beverages is seamless, offering options like the Vanilla Apple Pie Moonshine and White Chocolate Shot. These recipes are not just about the flavors but also about the experience, bringing a sense of occasion to every sip. Whether it's the visual appeal of layered shots or the unexpected combinations found in recipes like the Sex With An Alligator, the cookbook ensures a memorable experience.

Ideal for beginners, the cookbook serves as a comprehensive guide to shot making, from the simplest two-ingredient recipes to more elaborate creations that require a bit of preparation. It's an invitation to explore the playful side of cocktails, perfect for hosting, celebrating, or simply enjoying the art of mixology.

This collection proves that with a little creativity and the right ingredients, the possibilities for making enjoyable and memorable shots are endless.

Contents

Chapter 1: Jell O Shot Recipes

***

1. Apple Cinnamon Party Shots

"This holiday shot is made with the combination of cinnamon schnapps and green apple gelatin."

Serving: 24 | Prep: 10m | Ready in: 3h10m

Ingredients

- 1 (3 oz.) package green apple flavored Jell-O® mix
- 1 cup boiling water
- 1/4 cup cold water
- 3/4 cup cinnamon schnapps

Direction

• Stir gelatin mix in boiling water for about 2 minutes until dissolved. Mix in schnapps and cold water then transfer to disposable cups that are shot-sized. Place in the refrigerator for about 3 hours until firm.

2. Berry Shooters

"Summer parties are fun with this gelatinous drink. Make sure to down these in one gulp!"

Serving: 20 | Prep: 5m | Ready in: 8m

Ingredients

- 1 (3 oz.) package tropical fruit-flavored Jell-O® mix
- 1 cup hot water
- 1 cup triple berry vodka

Direction

- In a medium bowl with boiling water, stir in gelatin mix until it dissolves; mix vodka. Transfer to mini paper cups and place in the refrigerator until set.

3. Black Forest Cake Jell-o® Shot

"Fancy but easy-to-make Jell-O® shots."

Serving: 16 | Prep: 10m | Ready in: 8h15m

Ingredients

- 1 cup boiling water
- 1 (3 oz.) package cherry-flavored gelatin (such as Jell-O®)
- 4 fluid oz. white rum
- 3 fluid oz. creme de cacao
- 1 fluid oz. vodka
- 16 maraschino cherries
- 1 cup whipped cream
- 1 tbsp. chocolate syrup, or to taste

Direction

• In a bowl, combine gelatin and boiling water together until the gelatin dissolves. In another bowl, stir vodka, crème de cacao, and white rum together; add into the gelatin mixture.
• In each shot glass, put one maraschino cherry and top with the gelatin mixture. Place in the refrigerator for 8 hours to overnight until set. Take the shots out of the refrigerator; add whipped cream and chocolate syrup on top.

Nutrition Information

- Calories: 84 calories;
- Total Carbohydrate: 10.7 g
- Cholesterol: 3 mg
- Total Fat: 0.9 g
- Protein: 0.6 g
- Sodium: 31 mg

4. Buttery Nipple Gourmet Pudding Shots

"These pudding shots should not just be enjoyed in college."

Serving: 12 | Prep: 15m | Ready in: 45m

Ingredients

- 1 3/4 cups cold milk
- 2 fluid oz. butterscotch schnapps
- 2 fluid oz. Irish cream liqueur (such as Bailey's®)
- 1 fluid oz. vodka
- 1 fluid oz. coffee-flavored liqueur (such as Kahlua®)
- 1 (3.4 oz.) package instant butterscotch pudding mix

Direction

- In a bowl, mix coffee-flavored liqueur, milk, vodka, schnapps, and Irish cream liqueur together; put in pudding mix then thoroughly blend. Scoop mixture in disposable shot cups. Place in the refrigerator for at least half an hour until chilled.

Nutrition Information

- Calories: 97 calories;
- Total Carbohydrate: 14.4 g

- Cholesterol: 3 mg
- Total Fat: 0.7 g
- Protein: 1.2 g
- Sodium: 139 mg

5. Caramel Apple Jell-o® Shots

"Serve these Jell-O® shots featuring caramel and real apples in any parties."

Serving: 40 | Prep: 20m | Ready in: 8h25m

Ingredients

• 10 small Granny Smith apples
• 1 tsp. fresh lemon juice, or as needed
• 1 (1 oz.) envelope instant caramel-flavored hot chocolate mix (such as Land O Lakes® Cocoa Classics®)
• 1/2 cup boiling water
• 1/2 cup coconut milk
• 1 (.25 oz.) package gelatin (such as Knox ®)
• 1/4 cup white sugar
• 2 drops yellow food coloring
• 1/2 cup butterscotch schnapps

Direction

• Halve the apples lengthwise. Hollow apples with a melon baller, keep just enough flesh so the shells can keep their form. To minimize browning, squeeze lemon juice all over the apples. Place the apple on a baking sheet.
• In a pot, mix boiling water and hot chocolate together off heat until smooth; mix in coconut milk. Sprinkle gelatin on top and let it stand untouched for 1-2 minutes.

• Put the pot on medium-low heat, mix the cocoa mixture and gelatin together; stir in sugar until dissolved. In the mixture drop yellow food coloring. Take off heat and let the mixture cool for a bit.
• Transfer the cocoa mixture in the prepared apple shells. Place in the refrigerator for 8 hours to overnight.
• Slice each apple half into four wedges then serve right away.

Nutrition Information

• Calories: 37 calories;
• Total Carbohydrate: 6.6 g
• Cholesterol: 0 mg
• Total Fat: 0.6 g
• Protein: 0.3 g
• Sodium: 5 mg

6. Caramel Apple Martini Pudding Shots

"Fun pudding shots for cookouts! Freeze these treats until ready to consume."

Serving: 12 | Prep: 10m | Ready in: 10m

Ingredients

• 3/4 cup milk
• 1 (3.4 oz.) package butterscotch instant pudding mix
• 1/2 cup sour apple schnapps (such as DeKuyper® Sour Apple Pucker ®)
• 2 tbsps. butterscotch schnapps (such as DeKuyper® Buttershots®)
• 2 tbsps. vodka
• 1 (8 oz.) container frozen whipped topping (such as Cool Whip®), thawed

Direction

• In a bowl, stir pudding mix and milk together until smooth; blend in vodka, butterscotch schnapps, and apple schnapps. Fold whipped topping in the pudding mixture until well combined. Scoop the mixture in disposable party shot cups or shot glasses.

Nutrition Information

- Calories: 148 calories;
- Total Carbohydrate: 18.2 g
- Cholesterol: 1 mg
- Total Fat: 5.1 g
- Protein: 0.7 g
- Sodium: 136 mg

7. Chocolate Pudding Shots

"A delicious substitute for the Jell-O® shots that is served in lidded cups with plastic spoons. Freeze."

Serving: 16 | Prep: 10m | Ready in: 10m

Ingredients

- 1 (3.9 oz.) package instant chocolate pudding mix
- 3/4 cup milk
- 1/4 cup vodka
- 1/2 cup Irish cream liqueur
- 1 (8 oz.) container frozen whipped topping, thawed

Direction

- In a bowl, whisk milk and pudding mix together using an electric hand mixer for 1-2 minutes until smooth and begins to thicken. Mix in Irish cream liqueur and vodka. Stir in whipped topping until smooth; transfer to sixteen small cups.

Nutrition Information

- Calories: 113 calories;
- Total Carbohydrate: 13.3 g
- Cholesterol: < 1 mg
- Total Fat: 3.9 g

- Protein: 0.7 g
- Sodium: 106 mg

8. French 75 Jell-o® Shots

"The fanciest cocktail I've ever tried."

Serving: 16 | Prep: 10m | Ready in: 8h10m

Ingredients

• 1 cup boiling water
• 1/2 (3 oz.) package lemon-flavored gelatin mix (such as Jell-O®)
• 1/4 cup gin
• 1 3/4 cups sparkling wine, divided
• 3 (.25 oz.) envelopes unflavored gelatin
• 1 drop red food coloring

Direction

• In a glass measuring cup, pour boiling water over lemon-flavored gelatin, stir to mix. Add in gin, stirring. Strain into sixteen 2-oz. cups. Place cups in muffin tins, tilted to one side.
• Store in refrigerator about 4 hours, until it sets.
• In a small pot, mix 1 1/4 cup sparkling wine and unflavored gelatin. Allow to sit for 3 minutes. Heat 3 to 5 minutes over low heat until gelatin is dissolved, stirring continuously. Stir in food coloring and remaining 1/2 cup wine to combine.
• Take off muffin tins from refrigerator. Place cups upright; add wine mixture over lemon mixture.
• Take back to the refrigerator and refrigerate for 4 hours until set.

Nutrition Information

- Calories: 65 calories;
- Total Carbohydrate: 5.5 g
- Cholesterol: 0 mg
- Total Fat: 0 g
- Protein: 1.4 g
- Sodium: 20 mg

9. Gourmet Chocolate-covered Cherry Jell-o® Shots

"Popular shots for staff parties."

Serving: 12 | Prep: 10m | Ready in: 4h10m

Ingredients

- 1 (6 oz.) package cherry-flavored gelatin (such as Jell-O®)
- 1 cup boiling water
- 1/2 cup vodka
- 1/2 cup chocolate liqueur (such as Godiva®)

Direction

- On a baking sheet that can fit inside the refrigerator, place twelve 2oz plastic cups.
- Gently stir water in a bowl with cherry-flavored gelatin until it dissolves. Stir in chocolate liqueur and vodka.
- Transfer the gelatin mixture in the prepared cups.
- Place in the refrigerator for at least 4hrs to overnight.

Nutrition Information

- Calories: 116 calories;
- Total Carbohydrate: 17.4 g
- Cholesterol: 0 mg

- Total Fat: 0 g
- Protein: 1.3 g
- Sodium: 65 mg

10. Gourmet Gelly Shots: Berry Berry Good

"Even the Smurfs will like these delicious shots!"

Serving: 12 | Prep: 10m | Ready in: 8h10m

Ingredients

- 1 cup boiling water
- 1 (6 oz.) package mixed berry-flavored Jell-O® mix
- 1 cup raspberry-flavored vodka (such as Smirnoff®)

Direction

- On a baking sheet, place twelve 2oz. plastic cups.
- In a bowl with gelatin mix, gradually pour boiling water while stirring; keep on stirring while adding raspberry-flavored vodka. Transfer in plastic cups.
- Place in the refrigerator for 8 hours to overnight until set.

Nutrition Information

- Calories: 94 calories;
- Total Carbohydrate: 12.1 g
- Cholesterol: 0 mg
- Total Fat: 0 g
- Protein: 1.3 g

• Sodium: 52 mg

11. Gourmet Gelly Shots: Grape And Jack

"Make staff parties exciting with these shots."

Serving: 12 | Prep: 10m | Ready in: 8h10m

Ingredients

- 1 cup boiling water
- 2 (6 oz.) boxes grape-flavored Jell-O® mix
- 1 cup Tennessee whiskey (such as Jack Daniels ®)

Direction

- On a baking sheet, place twelve 2oz. plastic cups.
- In a bowl with gelatin mix, gradually pour boiling water while stirring. Keep on stirring while pouring in whiskey. Transfer mixture in plastic cups.
- Place in the refrigerator for 8 hours to overnight until set.

Nutrition Information

- Calories: 150 calories;
- Total Carbohydrate: 24.5 g
- Cholesterol: 0 mg
- Total Fat: 0 g
- Protein: 2.6 g

- Sodium: 104 mg

12. Gourmet Gelly Shots: Green Melon Goodness

"These shots are great for staff parties."

Serving: 12 | Prep: 10m | Ready in: 8h10m

Ingredients

- 1 cup boiling water
- 1 (6 oz.) package lime-flavored Jell-O® mix
- 1/2 cup vodka
- 1/2 cup melon liqueur (such as Midori®)

Direction

- On a baking sheet, put twelve 2oz. plastic cups.
- In a bowl with gelatin mix, gradually add boiling water while stirring. Pour in melon liqueur and vodka while continuously stirring. Transfer mixture in plastic cups.
- Place in the refrigerator for 8 hours to overnight until set.

Nutrition Information

- Calories: 111 calories;
- Total Carbohydrate: 16.8 g
- Cholesterol: 0 mg
- Total Fat: 0 g

- Protein: 1.3 g
- Sodium: 65 mg

13. Gourmet Gelly Shots: Malibu Goodness

"Tasty Caribbean-inspired shots."

Serving: 12 | Prep: 10m | Ready in: 8h10m

Ingredients

- 1 cup boiling water
- 1 (6 oz.) box strawberry-banana-flavored Jell-O® mix
- 1 cup coconut-flavored rum (such as Malibu®)

Direction

- On a baking sheet, place twelve 2oz. plastic cups.
- In a bowl with gelatin mix, gradually pour boiling water while stirring. Keep on stirring while pouring in rum. Transfer mixture in plastic cups.
- Place in the refrigerator for 8 hours to overnight until set.

Nutrition Information

- Calories: 104 calories;
- Total Carbohydrate: 15.8 g
- Cholesterol: 12 mg
- Total Fat: 1.6 g
- Protein: 2.2 g

- Sodium: 64 mg

14. Gourmet Gelly Shots: Orange Margarita!

"Margaritas can be enjoyed even without using a glass."

Serving: 12 | Prep: 10m | Ready in: 8h10m

Ingredients

- 1 cup boiling water
- 1 (6 oz.) package cherry Jell-O®
- 1/2 cup tequila
- 1/4 cup triple sec
- 1/4 cup orange liqueur (such as Grand Marnier®)

Direction

- In a baking sheet, place twelve 2oz plastic cups.
- While mixing, gradually pour boiling water on a bowl with gelatin mix. Keep on whisking while pouring in orange liqueur, triple sec, and tequila. Transfer mixture in plastic cups.
- Place in the refrigerator for 8 hours to overnight until set.

Nutrition Information

- Calories: 109 calories;
- Total Carbohydrate: 16.6 g

- Cholesterol: 0 mg
- Total Fat: 0 g
- Protein: 1.3 g
- Sodium: 65 mg

15. Halloween Candy Corn Jell-o® Shots

"Serve these seasonal boozy shots with candy corn, but remember to drink responsibly."

Serving: 16 | Prep: 15m | Ready in: 3h45m

Ingredients

- 1 1/2 cups boiling water, divided
- 1 (3 oz.) package lemon-flavored gelatin mix (such as Jell-O®)
- 2 cups vodka, divided
- ice cubes
- 1 (3 oz.) package orange-flavored gelatin mix (such as Jell-O®)
- 2 tbsps. warm water
- 1 (.25 oz.) envelope unflavored gelatin
- 1 (14 oz.) can sweetened condensed milk
- 1/2 cup light rum

Direction

- In a small bowl, stir lemon gelatin mix and 3/4 cup boiling water together until the gelatin dissolves. In a glass measuring cup, pour in 1 cup of vodka; put in enough ice until it reaches 1 1/4 cup. Mix with the lemon gelatin until thick; get rid of the unmelted ice. In tall shot glasses, pour in lemon gelatin mixture until 1/3 full.
- Place in the refrigerator for at least 1 1/2 hour until the gelatin layer sets.

• In a small bowl, stir orange gelatin mix and the remaining 3/4 cup boiling water together until the gelatin dissolves. In a glass measuring cup, pour in the remaining cup of vodka; put in enough ice until it reaches 1 1/4 cup. Mix with the orange gelatin until a bit thick; get rid of the unmelted ice. Pour on top of the lemon gelatin layer.
• Place in the refrigerator for at least 1 1/2hour until the gelatin layer sets.
• In a bowl, stir unflavored gelatin and 2tablespoons warm water together until the gelatin dissolves. Mix in rum and condensed milk; add on top of the orange gelatin layer.
• Place in the refrigerator for at least half an hour until the top layer sets.

Nutrition Information

• Calories: 202 calories;
• Total Carbohydrate: 22.4 g
• Cholesterol: 8 mg
• Total Fat: 2.1 g
• Protein: 3.3 g
• Sodium: 81 mg

16. Jenny's Amazing Vegan/vegetarian 'jello' Shots

"Enjoy this party-favorite treat in an easy way!"

Serving: 1 | Prep: 10m | Ready in: 45m

Ingredients

• 1 orange-flavored gel dessert snack (such as Snack Pack Juicy Gels®)
• 1 1/2 fluid oz. peach schnapps

Direction

• Take the gel dessert out of the plastic cup then put on a microwaveable bowl; use a fork to mash the gel dessert. Microwave on low until melted for 1-2 minutes and in ten-second intervals; mash occasionally with a fork. Mix in peach schnapps then transfer to shot cups. Place in the refrigerator for at least half an hour until set.

Nutrition Information

• Calories: 259 calories;
• Total Carbohydrate: 43.9 g
• Cholesterol: 0 mg
• Total Fat: 0.1 g

- Protein: 0 g
- Sodium: 38 mg

17. Key Lime Pie Jell-o® Shots

"Delicious Jell-O® shots that are just like small key lime pies with whipped cream on top."

Serving: 24 | Prep: 15m | Ready in: 4h15m

Ingredients

• 6 graham crackers
• 1/4 cup butter, melted, or more to taste
• 1 tsp. white sugar
• 1 (3 oz.) package lime-flavored gelatin mix (such as Jell-O®)
• 1 package unflavored gelatin (such as Knox®)
• 1 cup boiling water
• 6 fluid oz. cake-flavored vodka
• 1/4 cup heavy whipping cream, or to taste

Direction

• In a food processor, to make crumbs pulse graham crackers. Put sugar and melted butter, process until it forms into a firm crust mixture that can hold its shape. Divide the crust evenly in a muffin tin with 24 cups; push the crust at the bottom and sides of each cup.
• In a bowl, combine unflavored gelatin and lime-flavored gelatin; stir in boiling water until the gelatin dissolves. Mix in vodka and enough heavy cream until it reaches the preferred color; transfer in the crusted muffin cups until full. Use a sheet of plastic wrap to cover. Place in the refrigerator for at least 4 hours until set.

Nutrition Information

- Calories: 71 calories;
- Total Carbohydrate: 6 g
- Cholesterol: 8 mg
- Total Fat: 3.2 g
- Protein: 0.9 g
- Sodium: 53 mg

18. Lava Lamps

"Who knew that gelatin shots and champagne can work well together?"

Serving: 4 | Prep: 2m | Ready in: 2h2m

Ingredients

- 1 (3 oz.) package red or blue colored instant Jell-O® mix
- 1 cup boiling water
- 1 cup vodka
- 1 (750 milliliter) bottle champagne

Direction

• Mix boiling water and gelatin mix together in a medium bowl for about 2 minutes until the gelatin dissolves; mix in vodka. Transfer to small portion cups or paper cups; refrigerate to chill for at least 2 hours until set.

• Add champagne in glasses. Using a fork, muddle the gelatin then add to the glass of champagne. Slightly stir to make some 'lava' movement. Drink responsibly.

19. Margarita Jell-o® Shots

"A yummy margarita-flavored Jell-O® shot recipe! There's a little bit of kick to it so if you want it to be a lot more pleasing to the taste, just replace a bit of the alcohol with water."

Serving: 15 | Prep: 5m | Ready in: 5h5m

Ingredients

- 1 cup boiling water
- 1 (3 oz.) package lime-flavored gelatin mix (such as Jell-O®)
- 1/3 cup tequila
- 1/3 cup triple sec
- 1/3 cup water
- 15 plastic shot glasses, or as needed

Direction

- In a bowl, mix the gelatin mix and boiling water together. Mix well until the gelatin has fully dissolved. Put in the triple sec, water and tequila. Give it another mix.
- Distribute the mixture evenly into the shot glasses. Keep it in the fridge for about 5 hours until the gelatin has set.

Nutrition Information

- Calories: 52 calories;
- Total Carbohydrate: 7.3 g
- Cholesterol: 0 mg
- Total Fat: 0 g
- Protein: 0.5 g
- Sodium: 27 mg

20. Mudslide Mousse Shots

"Delicious chocolate pudding with cookies and whipped cream on top."

Serving: 12 | Prep: 20m | Ready in: 20m

Ingredients

- 1 tbsp. hot water
- 2 tsps. instant espresso powder
- 1 1/2 cups skim milk
- 1 (1.4 oz.) package instant sugar-free chocolate pudding mix
- 1 1/2 cups fat-free whipped topping, divided
- 16 chocolate wafer cookies, crumbled

Direction

- In a small bowl of hot water, mix in espresso powder until it dissolves; let it cool to room temperature.
- In a bowl, combine pudding mix and skim milk; stir in espresso mixture and fold in half cup of whipped topping.
- Scoop 2 tbsps. pudding in every shot glass; add 2 tsps. cookie crumbs, 2 tbsps. pudding, then 2 more tsps. cookie crumbs on top. Place a tbsp. of whipped topping on the very top.

Nutrition Information

- Calories: 71 calories;
- Total Carbohydrate: 13 g
- Cholesterol: < 1 mg
- Total Fat: 1.2 g
- Protein: 1.7 g
- Sodium: 159 mg

21. Oreo® Cookie Gourmet Pudding Shots

"Who say's pudding shots are only for college jocks?"

Serving: 12 | Prep: 10m | Ready in: 40m

Ingredients

• 1 cup cold milk
• 3/4 cup cake-flavored vodka (such as UV®)
• 1 (4 oz.) package cookies and cream instant pudding mix (such as Jell-O® Oreo®)
• 1 (8 oz.) container frozen whipped topping (such as Cool Whip®), thawed

Direction

• In a bowl, whisk pudding mix, vodka, and milk together until thick; fold in whipped topping. Scoop mixture in disposable cups; place in the refrigerator for at least half an hour until chilled.

Nutrition Information

• Calories: 140 calories;
• Total Carbohydrate: 13.7 g
• Cholesterol: 2 mg

- Total Fat: 5.4 g
- Protein: 0.9 g
- Sodium: 131 mg

22. Pina Colada Pudding Shots!

"This drink is really easy to make. Great for parties."

Serving: 24 | Prep: 10m | Ready in: 40m

Ingredients

• 1/2 cup milk
• 1/2 cup vodka (such as Smirnoff®)
• 1/2 cup pineapple rum (such as Malibu®)
• 1 (3.5 oz.) package instant coconut cream pie pudding mix
• 1 (8 oz.) container frozen whipped topping (such as Cool Whip®), thawed

Direction

• In a bowl, mix pineapple rum, milk, pudding mix, and vodka together; stir in whipped topping until it has a pudding-like consistency. Scoop in shot glasses. Place in the refrigerator for at least half an hour until set.

Nutrition Information

• Calories: 71 calories;
• Total Carbohydrate: 6.2 g
• Cholesterol: < 1 mg
• Total Fat: 2.6 g
• Protein: 0.3 g

- Sodium: 47 mg

23. Pineapple Peach Jell-o® Shots

"These Jell-O® shots are always a hit in every party."

Serving: 8 | Prep: 5m | Ready in: 3h15m

Ingredients

- 1 cup lemon-lime soda (such as Sprite®)
- 1 (3 oz.) package pineapple-flavored gelatin mix (such as Jell-O®)
- 3/4 cup peach schnapps
- 1/4 cup cold water

Direction

- On medium heat, simmer soda in a medium saucepan; stir in pineapple gelatin mix until it fully dissolves.
- Take off heat; mix in cold water and peach schnapps. Let it cool for 5-10 minutes until lukewarm.
- Transfer to 2oz. cups. Place in the refrigerator for 3-4 hours until set.

Nutrition Information

- Calories: 131 calories;
- Total Carbohydrate: 22.5 g
- Cholesterol: 0 mg
- Total Fat: 0.1 g
- Protein: 1 g

- Sodium: 44 mg

24. Pink Brain Shooter

"You can use water instead of peach schnapps to make this Halloween treat kid-friendly."

Serving: 12 | Prep: 20m | Ready in: 5h20m

Ingredients

- 1 brain-shaped gelatin mold
- 4 (3 oz.) packages peach flavored Jell-O® mix
- 3 cups boiling water
- 1 (12 fluid oz.) can evaporated milk
- 1 1/2 cups peach schnapps
- 4 drops blue food coloring
- 2 drops red food coloring
- 2 tsps. water

Direction

- Lightly grease a gelatin mold that is shaped like a brain.
- In a bowl with boiling water, mix in peach gelatin mix until it dissolves; cool to room temperature for about 20minutes. Stir in peach schnapps and evaporated milk; transfer mixture in the prepared mold. Place in the refrigerator for 4-6 hours until set.
- Submerge the mold in a very warm water to loosen but don't let it go inside the mold's top; turn the mold on a serving plate then lift to drop the brain. In a small bowl, combine 2 tsps. of water, red food coloring and blue food coloring. Paint the mixture on the brain's

grooves using a small and clean paintbrush. Refrigerate the brain until the color sets. Serve cold.

Nutrition Information

- Calories: 252 calories;
- Total Carbohydrate: 41.1 g
- Cholesterol: 9 mg
- Total Fat: 2.5 g
- Protein: 4.8 g
- Sodium: 141 mg

25. Pudding Shots

"Ditch the usual gelatin shots and serve this special and delicious drink instead."

Serving: 15 | Prep: 15m | Ready in: 45m

Ingredients

- 1 cup milk
- 1/2 cup Irish cream liqueur (eg. Bailey's®)
- 1/2 cup vodka (eg. Smirnoff®)
- 1 (4 serving size) package instant chocolate pudding mix

Direction

• In a bowl, stir instant pudding mix, milk, vodka, and Irish cream liqueur together until well blended; keep on mixing for 2 minutes.
• Scoop the pudding mixture in disposable party shot cups or shot glasses. Place in the refrigerator to chill for about half an hour until set; it will have a mousse-like consistency.

26. Raspberry Party Shots

"Parties are more wonderful with these raspberry vodka gelatin shooters."

Serving: 10 | Prep: 20m | Ready in: 1h25m

Ingredients

• 1 (6 oz.) package raspberry flavored Jell-O® mix
• 2 cups boiling water
• 3/4 cup ice water
• 1 1/4 cups raspberry vodka

Direction

• Mix boiling water and gelatin together until the gelatin dissolves; stir in vodka and ice water. Transfer to shot glasses or any container for party shots. Place in the refrigerator to chill for 1-2 hours until set.

27. Red Bull® And Vodka Jelly Shots

"To make these jelly shooters even better, you can use your preferred flavored vodka."

Serving: 16 | Prep: 5m | Ready in: 6h21m

Ingredients

• cooking spray
• 16 fluid oz. citrus-flavored energy drink (such as Red Bull®)
• 4 (.25 oz.) packages unflavored gelatin
• 2 cups cold vodka

Direction

• Using a cooking spray, lightly coat an 8-inch square baking pan.
• On medium-high heat, boil the energy drink in a heavy bottom pot; turn to a gentle simmer. Mix in gelatin for 1-2 minutes until it dissolves completely; take off heat. Slightly cool for about 10 minutes.
• Combine the gelatin mixture and vodka; transfer to the greased baking pan.
• Place the gelatin mixture in the refrigerator for about 6 hours until set. To slice the gelatin easily into 2-inch squares using a knife ran in hot water.

Nutrition Information

- Calories: 87 calories;
- Total Carbohydrate: 3.4 g
- Cholesterol: 0 mg
- Total Fat: 0 g
- Protein: 1.5 g
- Sodium: 28 mg

28. Rumchata® Pudding Shots

"You can enjoy these treats as an after-dinner dessert. These are much better than the usual Jell-O® shots."

Serving: 15 | Prep: 15m | Ready in: 3h15m

Ingredients

• 1 cup milk
• 1 cup rum cream liqueur (such as RumChata®)
• 1 (4 oz.) package instant chocolate pudding mix
• 1 (8 oz.) container frozen whipped topping (such as Cool Whip®), thawed

Direction

• In a bowl, stir pudding mix, rum liqueur, and milk together until thick; slowly mix in whipped topping. Scoop mixture in disposable shot cups. Arrange the cups on a plate. Place in the freezer for at least 3 hours until set and chilled.

Nutrition Information

• Calories: 84 calories;
• Total Carbohydrate: 10.8 g
• Cholesterol: 1 mg

- Total Fat: 4.2 g
- Protein: 0.9 g
- Sodium: 117 mg

29. Sliced Watermelon Jell-o® Shots

"Instead of vodka, you can add a cup of cold water in these tiny watermelon slices for the kids."

Serving: 20 | Prep: 30m | Ready in: 3h

Ingredients

- 5 limes
- 1 (3 oz.) package watermelon-flavored gelatin mix
- 1 cup boiling water
- 1 cup vodka
- 1 tsp. black sesame seeds, or as needed

Direction

• Halve the limes crosswise. Squeeze juice from the limes then reserve. Twist the lime rinds until inside out; scoop out the flesh and membranes. Make small cups by turning the peels back until the green rind is on the exterior again. In a small dish, arrange the lime halves with the edges together to keep them upright.

• In a bowl of boiling water, mix in watermelon gelatin mix until dissolved; cool the mixture to room temperature then mix in vodka. Transfer the gelatin mixture in prepared lime cups. Place in the refrigerator for 2-4 hours until set.

• Slice wedges from the lime cups with a sharp knife; add black sesame seeds on top.

Nutrition Information

- Calories: 49 calories;
- Total Carbohydrate: 5.5 g
- Cholesterol: 0 mg
- Total Fat: 0.1 g
- Protein: 0.5 g
- Sodium: 11 mg

30. Strawberry Cheesecake Jell-o® Shots

"The graham layer in these delicious, velvety, and adorable shots makes it even better."

Serving: 12 | Prep: 20m | Ready in: 1h50m

Ingredients

- 6 graham crackers
- 2 tbsps. melted butter
- 1 tsp. white sugar
- 1 (.25 oz.) package unflavored gelatin
- boiling water
- 1 (12 oz.) container whipped cream cheese
- 1/3 cup confectioners' sugar, or more to taste
- 1/2 tsp. vanilla extract
- 1 1/2 cups vodka, divided
- 1/2 (3 oz.) package strawberry flavored gelatin (such as Jell-O®)
- 1/4 cup boiling water
- 3 ice cubes

Direction

• In a food processor or blender, process the graham crackers until crushed; blend in sugar and melted butter until evenly incorporated. Gently push the graham cracker mix in twelve tall shot glasses.

• In a bowl, combine a quarter cup of boiling water and unflavored gelatin together until well blended.
• In a blender, pulse the gelatin mixture, cream cheese, vanilla extract, and confectioners' sugar together for a few times; blend in 1 cup of vodka until smooth. Add more confectioners' sugar according to taste. On top of the graham cracker layer, spread the cream cheese mixture leaving about 1 inch of space on top. Place in the refrigerator for at least 1 hour.
• In a bowl, combine a quarter cup of boiling water and strawberry gelatin together until well blended; put in ice cubes and the remaining half cup of vodka. Mix until the mixture starts to thicken and the ice is melted; pour on top of the cream cheese layer. Refrigerate shots for at least half an hour.

Nutrition Information

• Calories: 225 calories;
• Total Carbohydrate: 13.6 g
• Cholesterol: 32 mg
• Total Fat: 10.6 g
• Protein: 2.7 g
• Sodium: 192 mg

31. Strawberry Mango Jell-o® Shots

"These flavorful Jell-O® shots can be tweaked according to your taste."

Serving: 16 | Prep: 10m | Ready in: 1h10m

Ingredients

- 1 cup boiling water
- 1 (3 oz.) package strawberry-flavored gelatin (such as Jell-O®)
- 1 (.25 oz.) package unflavored gelatin (such as Knox ®)
- 2/3 cup cold water
- 1/3 cup mango-flavored rum

Direction

- In a bowl, stir unflavored gelatin, strawberry-flavored gelatin, and boiling water together until the gelatin dissolves; stir in mango-flavored rum and cold water. Transfer to 1oz. paper or plastic cups.
- Place in the refrigerator for about 1 hour until set.

Nutrition Information

- Calories: 31 calories;
- Total Carbohydrate: 4.5 g
- Cholesterol: 0 mg

- Total Fat: 0 g
- Protein: 0.9 g
- Sodium: 23 mg

32. Tainted Fruit Jell-o® Shots

"A different twist for your usual Jell-O® shots."

Serving: 20 | Prep: 15m | Ready in: 1h45m

Ingredients

• 1 (6 oz.) package pineapple-flavored gelatin mix (such as Jell-O®)
• 2 cups boiling water
• 1 (16 oz.) can pineapple chunks in juice
• 6 fluid oz. strawberry vodka
• 4 fluid oz. banana rum
• 1/2 cup cold water
• 20 mini plastic cups

Direction

• Combine boiling water and pineapple gelatin until it dissolves.
• Draw off juice from the pineapple, saving a quarter cup. Stir juice, cold water, rum, and vodka with the gelatin mixture.
• In each cup, put one chunk of pineapple then top with the gelatin mixture. Place in the refrigerator for 1 hour. Let it freeze for at least half an hour then serve.

Nutrition Information

• Calories: 74 calories;
• Total Carbohydrate: 11.8 g

- Cholesterol: 0 mg
- Total Fat: 0 g
- Protein: 0.9 g
- Sodium: 32 mg

33. Tainted Fruit Shots

"Delicious Jello with vodka and a bit of a kick."

Serving: 20 | Prep: 5m | Ready in: 1h

Ingredients

- 1 (6 oz.) package fruit flavored Jell-O® mix
- 2 cups boiling water
- 1 1/4 cups vodka, chilled
- 3/4 cup cold water

Direction

• Stir gelatin and boiling water together in a big bowl until the gelatin dissolves; mix in cold water and vodka. Transfer to plastic shot glasses; place in the refrigerator for 1 hour or until set.

34. Tart Lemon Drop Jelly Shots

"Enjoy these tasty alcoholic treats in moderation!"

Serving: 50 | Prep: 10m | Ready in: 6h45m

Ingredients

- 4 cups water
- 8 large lemons, cut into 8 wedges each
- 3 1/2 cups white sugar
- 8 (.25 oz.) packages unflavored gelatin
- 4 cups lemon vodka
- 1 tbsp. turbinado sugar

Direction

- On medium heat, simmer white sugar, lemon wedges, and water together until the sugar dissolves; regularly mash the lemons to let out oils and juice.
- Cook the mixture for another 5 minutes while stirring. Take off heat and cool for a bit. Remove the lemon pieces in the pot.
- Add gelatin in the pot.
- On low heat, heat gelatin mixture and syrup together for 5-10 minutes until dissolved.
- Take off heat; set aside for 15 minutes to let the mixture cool; stir in lemon vodka.
- Transfer mixture in a 9-inch by 13-inch baking pan. Place in the refrigerator for at least 6 hours until set.

• Pass a sharp knife in hot water. Slice the gelatin into cubes and dust with turbinado sugar. Serve.

Nutrition Information

• Calories: 106 calories;
• Total Carbohydrate: 16.2 g
• Cholesterol: 0 mg
• Total Fat: 0.1 g
• Protein: 1.2 g
• Sodium: 4 mg

35. Top Shelf Sparkling Margarita Jell-o®

"A flavorful, salty, tart, and sweet imitation of cold margarita for adults. Add lime wedge on top to serve."

Serving: 24 | Prep: 15m | Ready in: 4h30m

Ingredients

- 3 (3 oz.) packages lime-flavored gelatin mix (such as Jell-O®)
- 1 (3 oz.) package lemon-flavored gelatin mix (such as Jell-O®)
- 2 1/2 cups boiling water
- 1 2/3 cups premium tequila
- 2/3 cup triple sec
- 2/3 cup brandy-based orange liqueur (such as Grand Marnier®)
- 1/2 cup sweetened lime juice
- 2 cups sparkling water
- 1 lime, zested
- 1 pinch margarita salt, or as needed

Direction

- In a bowl with boiling water, mix in lemon gelatin and lime gelatin until completely dissolved. Refrigerate to chill for 15 minutes.
- Combine the gelatin mixture, tequila, sweetened lime juice, orange liqueur, and triple sec; softly mix in sparkling water. Transfer mixture

in twenty-four small cups; add lime zest in each cup. Place in the refrigerator for 4 hours until set. Sprinkle margarita salt in each cup then serve.

Nutrition Information

- Calories: 144 calories;
- Total Carbohydrate: 20 g
- Cholesterol: 0 mg
- Total Fat: 0 g
- Protein: 1.3 g
- Sodium: 69 mg

36. White Russian Pudding Shot

"Serve this fun and peculiar drink in cookouts!"

Serving: 12 | Prep: 10m | Ready in: 10m

Ingredients

• 3/4 cup milk
• 1 (3.4 oz.) package instant vanilla pudding mix
• 1/4 cup vodka
• 1/2 cup coffee-flavored liqueur (such as Kahlua®)
• 1 (8 oz.) container frozen whipped topping (such as Cool Whip®), thawed

Direction

• In a bowl, mix pudding mix and milk together with an electric mixer until thick. Combine pudding with coffee-flavored liqueur and vodka; fold in whipped topping. In shot glasses, scoop or pipe the pudding mixture. Store in the freezer until ready to serve.

Nutrition Information

• Calories: 145 calories;
• Total Carbohydrate: 16.3 g
• Cholesterol: 1 mg
• Total Fat: 5.1 g
• Protein: 0.7 g

• Sodium: 126 mg

Chapter 2: More Amazing Shot Recipes

***

37. Apple Jack Shot

"Are you ready for this shot?"

Serving: 1 | Prep: 5m | Ready in: 5m

Ingredients

- 1 fluid oz. whiskey
- 1 fluid oz. sour apple schnapps

Direction

- In a shot glass, put in whiskey then the sour apple schnapps; serve.

38. Apple Pie Shot

"Swish this delicious vodka shot in your mouth before swallowing, it tastes like apple pie!"

Serving: 1 | Prep: 1m | Ready in: 1m

Ingredients

- 1 fluid oz. vodka
- 1 fluid oz. apple cider
- 1 tbsp. whipped cream
- 1 pinch ground cinnamon

Direction

- Mix apple cider and vodka together in a 2oz. shot glass; add a dollop of whipped cream on top. Add a pinch of cinnamon.

39. B-52 Bomber

"This festive drink is made with the perfect combination of Irish cream, orange, and coffee."

Serving: 1 | Prep: 1m | Ready in: 1m

Ingredients

- 1 tbsp. Kahlua or other coffee flavored liqueur
- 1 tbsp. brandy-based orange liqueur (such as Grand Marnier®)
- 1 tbsp. Irish cream liqueur

Direction

- In a cordial glass, slowly pour coffee liqueur then the Grand Marnier. Gently add the Irish cream liqueur on top to prevent the liquids from blending.

40. B-52 Cocktail

"This layered drink will definitely throw you away."

Serving: 1 | Prep: 5m | Ready in: 5m

Ingredients

- 1/2 fluid oz. coffee-flavored liqueur (such as Kahlua®)
- 1/2 fluid oz. Irish cream liqueur (such as Bailey's®)
- 1/2 fluid oz. triple sec

Direction

- In a shot glass, add coffee liqueur then gently pour in Irish cream liqueur so it gloats on top. Add triple sec on the surface to make it float too and to make a drink with 3 layers.

Nutrition Information

- Calories: 162 calories;
- Total Carbohydrate: 19.1 g
- Cholesterol: 0 mg
- Total Fat: 0.1 g
- Protein: 0 g
- Sodium: 3 mg

41. Baby Guinness

"These tasty shooters are like small pints of Guinness."

Serving: 1 | Prep: 1m | Ready in: 1m

Ingredients

• 2 fluid oz. coffee flavored liqueur
• 1/2 fluid oz. Irish cream liqueur

Direction

• Pour coffee liqueur in a shot glass until almost full; add Irish cream on top. To form your shot's "head" the cream should stay floating on the surface.

42. Barenmeister

"This sweet shooter is made with the perfect combination of herbal liquors and German honey."

Serving: 1 | Prep: 5m | Ready in: 5m

Ingredients

- 1/2 (1.5 fluid oz.) jigger honey liqueur
- 1/2 (1.5 fluid oz.) jigger jagermeister liqueur

Direction

- In a shot glass, put jagermeister liqueur and honey liqueur; down in one go.

43. Big Kids' Watermelon

"Simple and delightful drink for adults. You can also make it using flavored-liquors like Absolut® Citron."

Serving: 20 | Prep: 5m | Ready in: 2days2h5m

Ingredients

- 1 large large watermelon
- 1 (750 milliliter) bottle spiced rum (such as Captain Morgan's®)

Direction

- With a paring knife, slice 6-inches deep and 4-6 inch diameter circle in the center of the watermelon; make a plug so you can tug it out. Gently pour in spiced rum inside the watermelon and let it absorb the rum. Repeat until all the spiced rum is gone. This can take a few hours.
- Place the plug back in the watermelon; use aluminum foil or plastic wrap to wrap the watermelon completely. Place in the refrigerator for 2-3 days.
- Unwrap and then cut the watermelon.

Nutrition Information

- Calories: 216 calories;
- Total Carbohydrate: 34 g

- Cholesterol: 0 mg
- Total Fat: 0.7 g
- Protein: 2.7 g
- Sodium: 5 mg

44. Bradley's Jagerbeer

"These Jagerbeers can be served in any size of glass. It's relatively easy to mix to make since it's only 50-50. Go easy with this drink!"

Serving: 1 | Prep: 5m | Ready in: 5m

Ingredients

• ice, as desired
• 1 fluid oz. Jagermeister liqueur
• 1 fluid oz. root beer

Direction

• Put ice in a small glass until full; stir in root beer and Jagermeister.

Nutrition Information

• Calories: 47 calories;
• Total Carbohydrate: 7.6 g
• Cholesterol: 0 mg
• Total Fat: 0 g
• Protein: 0 g
• Sodium: 6 mg

45. Brain Hemorrhage (halloween Alcohol Drink)

"Enjoy Halloween parties with these creepy and fun drinks. You can also mix strawberry schnapps if you want."

Serving: 1 | Prep: 5m | Ready in: 5m

Ingredients

- 1 fluid oz. chilled peach schnapps
- 1 tsp. chilled Irish cream liqueur (such as Bailey's®)
- 1 splash chilled grenadine syrup

Direction

- In a shot glass, add schnapps.
- Slowly add Irish cream liqueur on top of the schnapps and wait until the Irish cream liqueur starts to curdle and clump just like a brain, just a few moments.
- Slowly add a little grenadine on top of the brain like blood.
- Let your guest enjoy this disgustingly-delicious drink.

Nutrition Information

- Calories: 192 calories;

- Total Carbohydrate: 32.2 g
- Cholesterol: 0 mg
- Total Fat: 0.1 g
- Protein: 0 g
- Sodium: 9 mg

46. Brass Monkey

"Coconut rum and pineapple juice floating with 151 rum - a great shooter for parties!"

Serving: 1 | Prep: 1m | Ready in: 1m

Ingredients

- 1 (1.5 fluid oz.) jigger coconut flavored rum
- 1 (1.5 fluid oz.) jigger pineapple juice
- 1/2 fluid oz. 151 proof rum

Direction

• Combine coconut rum and pineapple juice in a cocktail mixer full of ice. Shake vigorously and strain into glass. Float 151 rum over the top. Drink in one gulp.

47. Buttery Nipple

"You can serve this treat as a drink or a shot."

Serving: 4 | Prep: 2m | Ready in: 2m

Ingredients

- 1 (1.5 fluid oz.) jigger vodka
- 1 (1.5 fluid oz.) jigger Irish cream liqueur
- 1 (1.5 fluid oz.) jigger butterscotch schnapps
- 1 (1.5 fluid oz.) jigger coffee flavored liqueur

Direction

• Put ice on a cocktail shaker until full; pour in coffee liqueur, vodka, butterscotch schnapps, and Irish cream. Shake the mixture well then filter into shot glasses. Serve.

48. Cb

"This indulgent chocolaty drink is made with vodka, coffee liqueur, and chocolate liqueur."

Serving: 3 | Prep: 2m | Ready in: 2m

Ingredients

- 1 cup chocolate liqueur
- 1 cup coffee flavored liqueur
- 1 cup vodka

Direction

• Mix vodka, coffee-flavored liqueur, and chocolate liqueur together in a lidded container; cover and place in the freezer. Pour in shot glasses. Stir and serve chilled.

49. Chocolate Cake Shot

"Every shot taste like chocolate cake!"

Serving: 1 | Prep: 5m | Ready in: 5m

Ingredients

- 1 fluid oz. hazelnut liqueur
- 1/2 fluid oz. vodka
- 1 lemon, cut into wedges
- white sugar

Direction

• Mix one part each of vodka and hazelnut liqueur in a shot glass; cover a lemon wedge with sugar. Suck the wedge and down the shot while the juice is still in your mouth.

50. Chocolate Covered Cherry Shooters

"This shot will remind you of cherry that is coated with chocolate."

Serving: 2 | Prep: 5m | Ready in: 5m

Ingredients

- 2 (1.5 fluid oz.) jiggers amaretto liqueur
- 1 tsp. grenadine syrup
- 2 tsps. chocolate syrup
- 2 tsps. heavy cream

Direction

- Put ice in a cocktail shaker until full; add heavy cream, amaretto, chocolate syrup, and grenadine syrup. Shake then filter into shot glasses.

51. Cough Syrup

"Smooth and soothing drink that's also known as Christmas in February. A good substitute for ginger brandy that is said to be a cure for whatever ails you."

Serving: 1 | Prep: 2m | Ready in: 2m

Ingredients

- 1 (1.5 fluid oz.) jigger creme de menthe liqueur
- 1 tsp. maraschino cherry juice
- 1 maraschino cherry

Direction

• Put crushed ice in an 8fl. oz. rocks glass until full. Stir in cherry juice and a shot of crème de menthe. Add cherry.

52. Fireman's Sour

"Parties are much more fun with this test tube drink that's a bit sweet and sour."

Serving: 6 | Prep: 5m | Ready in: 5m

Ingredients

- 4 fluid oz. rum
- 3 fluid oz. lime juice
- 1 fluid oz. grenadine syrup
- 1 fluid oz. simple syrup

Direction

- In a cocktail shaker with ice, pour simple syrup, rum, grenadine, and lime juice; secure lid and shake until the outside of shaker is frosted. Filter into shot glasses or clean test tubes to serve.

53. Flaming Doctor Pepper I

"Guzzle down this shooter carefully. The 151 rum can be brutal."

Serving: 1 | Prep: 5m | Ready in: 5m

Ingredients

• 1 cup beer
• 1 fluid oz. amaretto liqueur
• 1/4 fluid oz. 151 proof rum

Direction

• Pour beer in a pint glass until halfway full.
• In a regular shot glass, add amaretto then slowly pour in 151 proof rum on top to float.
• Fire up the shot by carefully touching it with an open flame. Drop the shot in the pint glass with beer; drink right away.

54. Flaming Doctor Pepper II

"Flaming drink that is almost like that carbonated drink. Down in big gulps!"

Serving: 1 | Prep: 2m | Ready in: 2m

Ingredients

- 2 fluid oz. amaretto liqueur
- 1/2 fluid oz. 151 proof rum
- 1 (1.5 fluid oz.) jigger beer

Direction

• In a highball glass, add amaretto then lightly slide in rum using the back of a spoon to make a layer. Light the rum carefully with a match then add beer. Let the flames die down then down in one go.

55. Green Gecko

"Get the night going with this alcoholic drink."

Serving: 2 | Prep: 1m | Ready in: 1m

Ingredients

• 1 (1.5 fluid oz.) jigger green Chartreuse
• 1 (1.5 fluid oz.) jigger 151 proof rum

Direction

• Put ice in a cocktail mixer until full; shake rum and Chartreuse together. Give it a vigorous shaking then filter drink in two shot glasses.

56. Grenade Launcher

"Make your night more exciting with this drink."

Serving: 1 | Prep: 1m | Ready in: 1m

Ingredients

- 3/4 fluid oz. peach schnapps
- 1/2 fluid oz. 151 proof rum

Direction

• Mix rum and peach schnapps together in a shot glass. Load the entire shot in your mouth then swallow.

57. Iowa City Oatmeal Cookie (cocktail)

"This delicious drink is a pub-favorite in Iowa."

Serving: 1 | Prep: 5m | Ready in: 5m

Ingredients

- 1/2 fluid oz. butterscotch schnapps
- 1/2 fluid oz. Irish cream liqueur
- 1/2 fluid oz. cinnamon schnapps
- 1/4 cup crushed ice

Direction

• Put crushed ice in a cocktail shaker; pour in cinnamon schnapps, Irish liqueur, and butterscotch schnapps. Shake then strain in a small glass.

Nutrition Information

- Calories: 161 calories;
- Total Carbohydrate: 20.1 g
- Cholesterol: 0 mg
- Total Fat: 0.1 g
- Protein: 0 g
- Sodium: 4 mg

58. Irish Car Bomb II

"St. Patrick's Day parties are fun with this chocolate milkshake-like drink."

Serving: 1 | Prep: 2m | Ready in: 2m

Ingredients

- 3/4 fluid oz. Irish whiskey
- 3/4 fluid oz. Irish cream liqueur
- 6 fluid oz. Irish stout beer

Direction

• Pour half each of Irish cream and Irish whiskey in a shot glass until full. In a pint glass, add Irish stout beer; release the shot glass and down the contents in one go.

59. Jager Bomb

"A tasty combination of Red Bull® Energy Drink and Jagermeister."

Serving: 1 | Prep: 5m | Ready in: 5m

Ingredients

• 1/2 (8.3 oz.) can citrus flavored energy drink (e.g. Red Bull™)
• 1 (1.5 fluid oz.) jigger Jagermeister liqueur

Direction

• In a pint glass, pour in energy drink; put Jagermeister in a shot glass. Toast then let the shot fall down in the pint glass. Drink up!

60. Kamikaze

"You can mix fresh juices in your Kamikazes if you want a little twist."

Serving: 1 | Prep: 2m | Ready in: 2m

Ingredients

- 1 fluid oz. vodka
- 1 fluid oz. orange liqueur

Direction

- In a shot glass, add orange-flavored liqueur and vodka; serve.

61. Kamikaze Shots For A Crowd

"An easy recipe for kamikaze shots."

Serving: 8 | Prep: 5m | Ready in: 5m

Ingredients

- 6 fluid oz. vodka
- 3 fluid oz. lime juice
- 3 fluid oz. triple sec

Direction

• In a cocktail shaker with ice, add triple sec, lime juice, and vodka; secure the lid and shake until the shaker is frosted. Filter into chilled shot glasses. Serve.

62. Layered Margarita Jell-o® Shots

"A traditional and colorful cocktail."

Serving: 12 | Prep: 10m | Ready in: 12h10m

Ingredients

• 2 1/2 cups boiling water, divided
• 1 (3 oz.) package lime-flavored gelatin mix (such as Jell-O®), divided
• 1 cup tequila, divided
• 2 (0.3 oz.) packages sugar-free orange gelatin mix (such as Jell-O®)
• 1/4 cup triple sec

Direction

• In a glass measuring cup, place 1/2 of the lime-flavored gelatin then stir in a cup of boiling water until the gelatin dissolves; mix in half cup tequila. Pour mixture in 12 two-oz. cups until 1/3 full.
• Place in the refrigerator for 4 hours until set.
• In a glass measuring cup, mix orange gelatin mixes and half cup boiling water together until the gelatin dissolves. Mix in Triple Sec. Take the cups out of the refrigerator. In each cup, layer the orange gelatin mixture until half as tall as the lime mixture.
• Place in the refrigerator for 4 hours until set.

• In a glass measuring cup, mix the remaining lime-flavored gelatin and a cup of boiling water together until the gelatin dissolves; mix in the remaining half cup tequila. Take the cups out of the refrigerator. Layer lime-tequila mixture over the cup as tall as the bottom layer.
• Place in the refrigerator for 4 hours until set.

Nutrition Information

• Calories: 88 calories;
• Total Carbohydrate: 8.4 g
• Cholesterol: 0 mg
• Total Fat: 0 g
• Protein: 0.7 g
• Sodium: 34 mg

63. Lemon Drop Shots

"Delicious shots that taste like candies."

Serving: 1 | Prep: 10m | Ready in: 10m

Ingredients

- 3/4 fluid oz. vodka (such as Absolut®)
- 3/4 fluid oz. lemon juice
- 2 1/2 tsps. white sugar, or to taste
- 1 lemon, cut into wedges

Direction

- In a shot glass, mix lemon juice and vodka together; top with half a tsp. of sugar.
- Put 2 tbsps. sugar in a small platter; plunge lemon wedges. Drink the shot then immediately suck on the sugar-coated lemon.

Nutrition Information

- Calories: 116 calories;
- Total Carbohydrate: 23.9 g
- Cholesterol: 0 mg
- Total Fat: 0.3 g
- Protein: 1.4 g
- Sodium: 4 mg

64. Liquid Cocaine

"Party shots made with peppermint schnapps, Jagermeister, and Goldschlager."

Serving: 1 | Prep: 5m | Ready in: 5m

Ingredients

- 1/2 fluid oz. cinnamon schnapps (i.e. Goldschlager™)
- 1/2 fluid oz. peppermint schnapps
- 1/2 fluid oz. Jagermeister liqueur

Direction

• In a frozen shot glass, pour Jagermeister, peppermint schnapps, and cinnamon schnapps. Drink up!

65. Mind Eraser

"This is a usual bar drink recipe with of the famous shots."

Serving: 1 | Prep: 5m | Ready in: 5m

Ingredients

- 1/4 cup coffee-flavored liqueur (such as Kahlua®)
- 1/4 cup lemon-lime soda (such as Sprite®)
- 1/4 cup vodka

Direction

• In an ice-filled cocktail glass or a shot glass, softly pour in coffee-flavored liqueur and lemon-lime soda in a layer. Gently pour in vodka on the top layer. Make sure to pour them in order and not combine the layers together before drinking. Use a straw to drink the layers.

66. Oatmeal Cookie

"This delicious drink should still be taken in moderation."

Serving: 1 | Prep: 1m | Ready in: 1m

Ingredients

- 1/2 fluid oz. butterscotch schnapps
- 1/2 fluid oz. Irish cream liqueur
- 1/2 fluid oz. jagermeister liqueur
- 1/2 fluid oz. cinnamon schnapps

Direction

• Put butterscotch schnapps and Irish cream on a layer in one shot glass; pour in Jagermeister then on top float with cinnamon schnapps.

Nutrition Information

• Calories: 178 calories;
• Total Carbohydrate: 22.3 g
• Cholesterol: 0 mg
• Total Fat: 0.2 g
• Protein: 0 g
• Sodium: 3 mg

67. Oyster Shooter

"Raw oyster shots with pepper vodka, horseradish, and hot sauce."

Serving: 4 | Prep: 5m | Ready in: 5m

Ingredients

- 4 shucked oysters
- 4 tsps. hot pepper sauce
- 1 tsp. prepared horseradish (optional)
- 1/4 cup vodka, or as needed

Direction

• Put an oyster in each shot glass; put one tsp. of hot sauce and horseradish in each glass to taste. Pour in vodka until full; drink right away.

68. Pan Galactic Gargle Blaster

"The best alcoholic drink in the cosmos."

Serving: 2 | Prep: 10m | Ready in: 10m

Ingredients

• 1 sugar cube
• 1 drop bitters
• 1/4 tsp. salt
• 1 3/4 tsps. warm water
• 3 fluid oz. gin
• 2 fluid oz. tequila
• 1 lemon-lime-flavored immune support effervescent tablet (such as Emergen-C®)
• 1 fluid oz. peppermint schnapps
• crushed ice, as desired
• 1 olive

Direction

• In a small vessel, put in a sugar cube and top with bitters. Let it immerse to make an Algolian suntiger tooth.
• To make the Santraginus V sea water, mix water and salt together in a concave apparatus.
• In a serving glass, mix tequila (O'l Janx Spirit), gin (Arcturan Mega-gin), and the Santraginus V sea water together; drop in the effervescent tablet (Fallion marsh gas). Over the back of the spoon set above the liquid's surface, pour in the Qualactin Hypermint.

• Pour into the concoction the Algolian Suntiger tooth and allow it to dissolve. Mix in ice (Zamphuor) until the temperature hits 0°C or 32°F. Add an olive on top. Drink carefully.

Nutrition Information

• Calories: 237 calories;
• Total Carbohydrate: 8.2 g
• Cholesterol: 0 mg
• Total Fat: 0.3 g
• Protein: 0 g
• Sodium: 315 mg

69. Peppermint Patty

"This can be a drink after dinner or a delicious dessert."

Serving: 1 | Prep: 5m | Ready in: 5m

Ingredients

• 2 ice cubes
• 2 fluid oz. coffee flavored liqueur
• 1 fluid oz. peppermint schnapps

Direction

• In a chilled rocks glass, put in ice cubes; add coffee liqueur then top with schnapps. Drink up!

70. Pumpkin Pie Pudding Shots

"Who says that Halloween nights can't be fun for adults? You're in for a treat with these pudding shots made exciting with spiced rum. You can also layer it with spaced wafer or graham crumbs"

Serving: 18 | Prep: 10m | Ready in: 20m

Ingredients

- 1 (15 oz.) can pumpkin puree
- 4 oz. cream cheese
- 1/2 tsp. ground cinnamon
- 1/8 tsp. ground nutmeg, or to taste
- 1 cup milk
- 3/4 cup spiced rum
- 1 (3 oz.) package instant vanilla pudding mix
- 1 (8 oz.) container frozen whipped topping, thawed

Direction

• In a bowl, beat nutmeg, pumpkin, cinnamon, and cream cheese together using an electric mixer until creamy and smooth. Stir in vanilla pudding mix, rum, and milk until blended; mix in whipped topping until combined.

• Place in the freezer for 10-15 minutes until set. In each glass, scoop in 2tablespoons of pudding.

Nutrition Information

- Calories: 115 calories;
- Total Carbohydrate: 10.1 g
- Cholesterol: 8 mg
- Total Fat: 5.5 g
- Protein: 1.2 g
- Sodium: 167 mg

71. Red Head

"This yummy cocktail drink can be made with whatever liquor that you have."

Serving: 1 | Prep: 5m | Ready in: 5m

Ingredients

• 1 fluid oz. Jagermeister liqueur
• 1/2 fluid oz. coffee liqueur, such as Kahlua
• 1/2 fluid oz. peach schnapps
• 1/2 fluid oz. cranberry juice
• 1/2 fluid oz. tomato juice

Direction

• In a cocktail shaker with ice, add tomato juice, Jagermeister, cranberry juice, coffee liqueur, and schnapps; secure lid and shake until the shaker is frosted. Filter into a small rocks glass. Serve.

72. Rickyrootbeer

"Everybody loves this unusual shot that tastes like you're drinking a root beer float."

Serving: 1 | Prep: 5m | Ready in: 5m

Ingredients

- 1/2 fluid oz. vanilla vodka
- 1/2 fluid oz. Irish cream liqueur
- 4 fluid oz. root beer

Direction

• In a shot glass, put Irish cream and vodka. In a tumbler, pour root beer. Plunge the shot glass in the tumbler with root beer; drink right away.

73. Sex With An Alligator

"A sweet and pleasing drink made with Jagermeister, coconut rum, raspberry liquor, melon liquor, and pineapple juice. This drink is also known a Sex with an alligator."

Serving: 1 | Prep: 5m | Ready in: 5m

Ingredients

- 2 (1.5 fluid oz.) jiggers pineapple juice
- 1/2 (1.5 fluid oz.) jigger melon liqueur
- 1/2 (1.5 fluid oz.) jigger coconut rum
- 1/2 (1.5 fluid oz.) jigger raspberry flavored liqueur
- 1/2 (1.5 fluid oz.) jigger jagermeister liqueur

Direction

- Fill a cocktail shaker with ice; pour in coconut rum, melon liqueur, and pineapple juice. Shake well then filter into a rocks glass. Let the raspberry liqueur sink at the bottom of the glass after pouring it; top with Jagermeister. If done properly, the top and bottom layer should be brown while the middle is green.

74. Slippery Nipples

"Brighten up parties and gatherings with these sweet but alcoholic shots."

Serving: 1 | Prep: 1m | Ready in: 1m

Ingredients

- 3/4 fluid oz. butterscotch schnapps
- 3/4 fluid oz. Irish cream liqueur

Direction

- In a shot glass, put 1/2 shot each of butterscotch schnapps and Irish cream until full.

75. Southern Ireland

"You can serve this drink in different ways, shake in a martini shaker with ice, as a shooter, or over ice. You can take it warm with hot chocolate and whipped cream."

Serving: 1 | Prep: 10m | Ready in: 10m

Ingredients

• 1 1/2 fluid oz. Irish cream liqueur (such as Baileys®)
• 1 1/2 fluid oz. peach-flavored bourbon liqueur (such as Southern Comfort ®)

Direction

• In a small glass, mix bourbon liqueur and Irish cream liqueur together.

Nutrition Information

• Calories: 277 calories;
• Total Carbohydrate: 20.7 g
• Cholesterol: 0 mg
• Total Fat: 0.1 g
• Protein: 0 g
• Sodium: 3 mg

76. Storm Trooper

"A change for your usual Jager shot!"

Serving: 1 | Prep: 5m | Ready in: 5m

Ingredients

- 1 fluid oz. Jagermeister liqueur
- 1 fluid oz. peppermint schnapps

Direction

- In a shot glass, add Jagermeister then top with schnapps. Drink up!

77. Strawberry Shooters

"Eat this messy but delightful treat all at once."

Serving: 20 | Prep: 10m | Ready in: 10m

Ingredients

- 1 (750 milliliter) bottle amaretto liqueur
- 1 (1 lb.) fresh strawberries, hulled and cored
- 1 (7 oz.) can whipped cream (such as Reddi-Whip®)

Direction

- In each strawberry, add amaretto liqueur and garnish with whipped cream.

Nutrition Information

- Calories: 151 calories;
- Total Carbohydrate: 16.9 g
- Cholesterol: 7 mg
- Total Fat: 2.3 g
- Protein: 0.3 g
- Sodium: 15 mg

78. Vanilla Apple Pie Moonshine

"You won't even notice the taste of alcohol in this drink that can be taken warm or cold. It tastes even better the longer it is stored in the jar."

Serving: 75 | Prep: 10m | Ready in: 1h30m

Ingredients

- 1 gallon apple juice
- 1 gallon apple cider
- 3 cups white sugar
- 1 cup brown sugar
- 12 cinnamon sticks
- 1 tsp. vanilla extract
- 2 whole cloves
- 1 (1 liter) bottle 151 proof grain alcohol (such as Everclear®)
- 2 cups cake-flavored vodka (such as UV®)

Direction

• In a big pot, boil cloves, apple juice, vanilla extract, apple cider, cinnamon sticks, white sugar, and brown sugar together. Turn to medium-low heat and let it simmer for about 20 minutes until the sugars dissolve. Take off heat and cool completely for about 1 hour.
• Mix vodka and grain alcohol in the apple juice blend. Get rid of the cinnamon sticks; let it stand. Transfer the moonshine in bottles. In each bottle, place one cinnamon stick then seal. Refrigerate.

Nutrition Information

- Calories: 144 calories;
- Total Carbohydrate: 23.4 g
- Cholesterol: 0 mg
- Total Fat: 0.1 g
- Protein: 0 g
- Sodium: 8 mg

79. Wenny's White Cake Shots

"After taking these festive shots, bite into lemon slices that are coated in sugar. It's like you're eating white cake!"

Serving: 4 | Prep: 5m | Ready in: 5m

Ingredients

• ice
• 2 fluid oz. vanilla-flavored vodka
• 2 fluid oz. hazelnut liqueur

Direction

• Put ice in a shaker until full; add hazelnut liqueur and vanilla-flavored vodka. Cover and shake until the shaker is chilled. Filter the contents in four shot glasses.

Nutrition Information

• Calories: 88 calories;
• Total Carbohydrate: 6.6 g
• Cholesterol: 0 mg
• Total Fat: 0 g
• Protein: 0 g
• Sodium: 3 mg

80. White Chocolate Shot

"Every girl's night is much more fun with these tasty smoothie shots."

Serving: 4 | Prep: 5m | Ready in: 5m

Ingredients

- 2 fluid oz. creme de cacao liqueur
- 2/3 cup French vanilla ice cream
- 1/4 cup sweetened whipped cream

Direction

- Blend ice cream and crème de cacao together in a blender until smooth; transfer to shot glasses then add whipped cream on top.

Printed in Great Britain
by Amazon

51110561R10077